AF808667

JOSEPHS, RISE UP!

A BIBLE-BASED VISION FOR NIGERIA'S ECONOMY

Homes of Love

For Scripture quotations from the NKJV unless otherwise mentioned
New King James Version®. Copyright © 1982 by Thomas Nelson.
Used by permission. All rights reserved.
Revised Standard Version RSV®, © 1947 1946, 1952, 1971 by the Division of Christian Education of the National Council of the Churches of Christ in the USA Used by permission. All rights reserved worldwide.

Copyright © 2017, Homes of Love, Kansas City, Missouri, USA
www.homes-of-love.com
All rights reserved. No part of this book can be reproduced, copied or distributed in printed or electronic form without authorization.
First edition: January 2017
Printed in USA
ISBN: 978-1-943202-05-8

JOSEPHS, RISE UP!

A BIBLE-BASED VISION FOR NIGERIA'S ECONOMY

Pierre Bezençon

TABLE OF CONTENTS

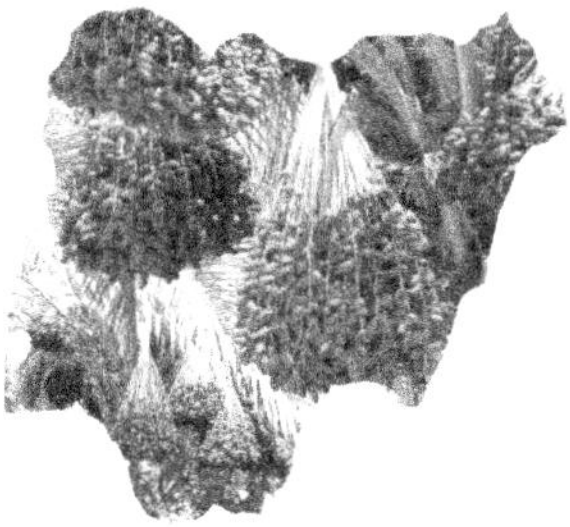

FOREWORD

Why would the cover of a book about Nigeria's economy have a picture with palm trees loaded with fruit?

Because a palm tree is a symbol of abundance, result of men's work and God's blessing.

The vision of this book is about providing everyone in the land with an abundant supply of food in a time of recession.

Palm trees and their fruit cover the whole map of Nigeria as a declaration that everyone is included.

This picture opens each chapter of the book to remind us that when men and God work hand in hand the harvest is plentiful.

To Pastor Samuel Olamilekan Adedeji
who loves God and his country Nigeria

THE VISION

As God raised up Joseph, son of Jacob, to provide food for his people in a time of severe famine. Today God has prepared (and is preparing) modern day "Josephs" (male and female) to provide the needed provision and solutions in a time of economic crisis.

Today it is not about one man. God will raise a large number of "Josephs" to impact and bless every aspect of the nation. Some "Josephs" will move on a national level, others on a state level, others on a city level and others on a neighborhood level, but the quality of their life will make a massive difference in Nigeria. Through them God will save many lives from poverty, sickness and malnutrition. The "Josephs" will contribute to the economic development of their country and to the wellbeing of a large part of the population.

The provision that the "Josephs" will bring to others will not be limited to contributing to charity or giving food to the hungry. They will create jobs, share their expertise, offer counsel, generate opportunities, share resources, train and advise young entrepreneurs, develop new energetic strategies, innovate in new services, encourage education and skill development, provide better health attention to the poor, inspire new low rate micro credit lending and even advance transport lines and digital communication routes. The "Josephs" will be known as problem solvers and solution givers.

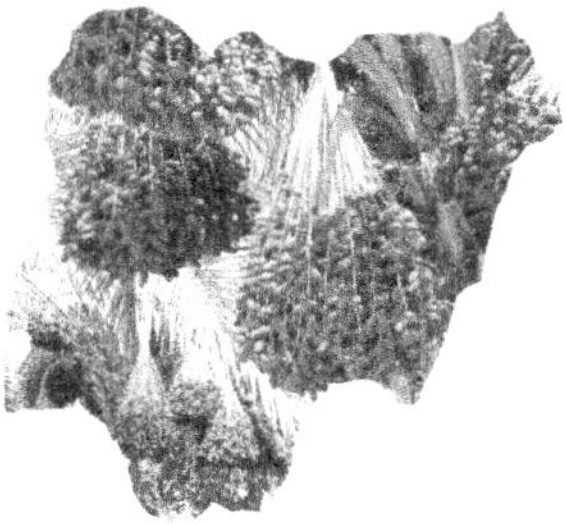

CHAPTER ONE

JOSEPH

Overview of Joseph's story and character's highlights

The whole story of Joseph, son of Jacob, is found in the Bible, in the book of Genesis, chapters 37 to 50. I would encourage you to read it afresh so you will benefit more from this book. I also invite you to check every reference and affirmation to make sure that all the teaching is Bible-based.

Joseph was his father's favorite (Genesis 37:3). Because of this he endured hatred, jealousy and treason from his brothers (Genesis 37:4; 37:11; 37:19-20). At age 17 he received some prophetic dreams about a position of honor and superiority among his relatives (Genesis 37:3). In his youthful **pride** and boldness he shared his dreams and his brothers' opposition intensified. He had to wait 20+ years to see the fulfillment of his God given dreams (Genesis 41:46; 42:9).

- Joseph was **loyal** to his father (Genesis 37:2; 37:13-14), to Potiphar, to God (Genesis 39:8-9) and later to Pharaoh (Genesis 47:14-21).
- He was **trustworthy** and people in authority entrusted him with much (Jacob, Potiphar, the jailer and Pharaoh).
- Joseph was **honest**. Potiphar and the jailer left all in his charge (Genesis 39:6; 39:23).
- Joseph was a **hard worker** (Genesis 39:3-6; 39:21; 39:22-23; 40:4; 41:46-49; 41:56)
- Joseph was tested by Potiphar's wife (sexual harassment at work by an authority figure). He was a man of **integrity** when facing pressure and temptation.
- Joseph was a man of **truth**. He dared tell the truth, either pleasant or unpleasant to the butler and the baker, as well as to Pharaoh.
- **God was with Joseph** in manifest ways so people could see it (Genesis 39:2-3; 39:21; 41:38). The Scriptures state clearly that the presence of God was the key to Joseph's success.
- **Joseph was with God** as we see him operating in several **gifts of the Spirit**: dreams (Genesis 37:6-9), the interpretation of dreams (Genesis 40:12; 40:18; 41:12-13; 41:25), discernment (Genesis 40:6-7), wisdom (Genesis 41:33-39), administration (Genesis 39:2-3; 39:22-23; 41:34-36; 41:47-49), the gift of faith (Genesis 40:8; 41:16; 41:25; 41:28; 41:36), leadership (Genesis 39:4-6), understanding (Genesis 45:5; 45:8; 50:20) and compassion (Genesis 45:15; 50:19-21).
- **Joseph consistently gave the glory to God for his spiritual gifts**. He did not take the credit for his God-given gifting for himself. He witnessed that his spiritual gifts came from God and all knew about it (Genesis 40:8; 41:16; 41:25; 41:28; 41:32; 41:38-39).

The key to Joseph's promotions

Joseph experienced three massive promotions: in Potiphar's house, later in the prison and then in Pharaoh's court. Each time it happened he was very low. The first time he was a beaten up slave arriving from a foreign land, the second time he was a slave charged with an alleged disgusting crime and, the third time, he was a Hebrew slave serving in a dirty prison.

But "***God was with Joseph***" (Genesis 39:1; 39:21; 41:38). Potiphar, the jailer and Pharaoh all saw that God was with Joseph. The reason for his three unlikely promotions was the manifest presence of God with him. These men did not know the true God but they were somehow able to see the living God moving powerfully in Joseph's life.

The constant presence of God in Joseph's life was not by accident. Relationship with God involves two-way communication. His presence is not given "randomly" or "by chance". God entrusts his presence and favor to those who seek His presence and walk in His ways. The "visible" presence of God in someone's life means that their relationship with Him has been cultivated, watered and maintained for years. Joseph, operating consistently in such an abundance and accuracy in spiritual gifts, speaks a lot about the depth and extent of his relationship with God. Joseph walked before God. Joseph lived his life in front of God. When Potiphar's wife tempted him he was able to reject her, because God was his audience when no one else was watching.

Joseph experienced two major "lows" before two major "highs"

- First, Joseph lost his father's affection, his family, his country, his language, his freedom, his culture, his rights and his status, when he was sold as a slave.
- Secondly, because of his faithfulness to God, Joseph lost his position, his promotion, his success and his reputation. He lost the favor he enjoyed and the little "freedom" he had as a privileged slave, when he was falsely accused of adultery and thrown into prison.

Joseph did not experience these "ups and downs" because he had done **something wrong**. He went through these heart wrenching times **because he did the right thing**. Joseph was persecuted because he was a righteous man. He did not suffer because he was unrighteous.

Through these "highs and lows" God was setting his heart free from any worldly matter (position, promotion, comfort, wealth, ambition, prestige, rank, honours and personal rights). Joseph lost everything twice, and he was restored to a new situation by the grace of God. He could not attach his heart to the things of this world. His only sure reality was God Himself. God was the only One that remained when everything else had been lost. Joseph was invited to trust Him to the uttermost and not rely on anyone else. He knew that God alone was his refuge, his strength, his treasure and his reward. His heart was trained to say "yes" to God in the midst of blessings and in the midst of trials. His long years of training prepared him to be faithful for the time of his national promotion. Through the "highs and lows" he had gained a steel resolve to remain faithful to his God whatever the circumstances.

God tries and tests the people He wants to use. **Before being entrusted with much we must be found faithful with little** (Mat 25:21; Luke 16:10). Joseph was being prepared for his high position through suffering (hatred, jealousy, violence, betrayal, slavery, foreignness, temptation, lies, false accusation, demotion, imprisonment and oblivion). He went from youthful pride to mature humility and forgiveness, even in his high position. He kept his relationship with God alive even when he was alone in a foreign land. He discerned what God was doing to rescue his people, and in so doing he avoided bitterness in his relationship with his brothers (Genesis 45:5; 45:8; 50:20). Joseph experienced a succession of promotions and demotions that tested his heart to be truly faithful, no matter the circumstances. The combination of adversities and privileges tests our character. This process builds an inner strength in the long-term and makes us eventually unmovable in our resolve to be faithful to God. Faithfulness is NOT learned when we are in a leadership position; it is learned beforehand, then applied.

Joseph's skills, profile and résumé

Joseph had an **entrepreneur's profile**. He knew how to **administrate goods and people**. He had the ability to organize and supervise (oversee) the work of others. He was able to **generate wealth with the help of God**. **He saw solutions where other people saw problems**. He had a vision about how to handle a national crisis (famine). He did not fear to do something that nobody had done before him: he led a seven year plan to gather the extra grain in storehouses to be built for the time of coming need. **Joseph provided the solution ahead of the problem** because God gave him insights into the future. He created jobs. He hired architects, masons, carpenters and all sorts of tradesmen to achieve his purpose. Joseph was **a visionary man gifted with divine wisdom** (Genesis 41:33-39), **a skilled economist** (Genesis 41:34), **a successful businessman** (Genesis 41:56; 42:6; 47:14-21) and **an international trader** (Genesis 41:57). He knew what the need of the people would be and he brought wise solutions.

Over the years he developed his skills. At first, he was able to **oversee**, and later he was able to **oversee the overseers** (Genesis 41:34 multi-level management). Joseph was also a good communicator (notice his concise accurate address to Pharaoh). He spoke at least **two languages fluently**. He was able to adjust perfectly to **two different cultures** (cross-cultural skills). He created a lot of jobs in the country and worked for the good of the nation. He was business minded: he did what he did for a profit. Rather than himself He **enriched** Pharaoh **the king,** which is a reference to KING Jesus the King, while avoiding massive starvation (Genesis 47:14-21).

Joseph lived a very comfortable life with horses and chariots (= modern day cars), enjoyed state honours, wore fine clothing and jewelry (Genesis 41:42-43), had a large well equipped house, ate choice food and had multiple servants, administrators and personal guards (Genesis 43:16; 43:19; 43:24; 43:30-34). But his personal wealth was nothing compared to the massive amount of wealth he transferred and accumulated for his king (reference to the KING). Joseph was working for his king and served his purposes loyally.

Note: Like most biblical figures Joseph was not a priest or a minister. He was a shepherd who became a modern day "minister of economy". God wants to use businessmen, businesswomen, doctors, engineers, mechanics, nurses, bankers and all sort of marketplace people that are not part of the clergy to advance His kingdom. He desires to bring practical solutions in times of crisis in order to bless His people.

God's care for Joseph

The details of Joseph's story show God's care for him and should encourage all the "Josephs" not to doubt the love of God for them, and never give up in the midst of times of preparation.

God always opened a small door of escape for Joseph. He was divinely preserved and protected from destruction: intervention of his brother Ruben (Genesis 37:21), absence of water in the pit (Genesis 37:24), wisdom of his brother Judah (Genesis 37:27-28), Potiphar's favor (Genesis 39:3), being thrown into prison instead of capital punishment (Genesis 39:20), the need of interpretation for Pharaoh dreams and absence of other interpreters of the dreams (Genesis 41:8), and the memories of the butler to bring Joseph out of the prison (Genesis 41:12).

God's sovereignty led the whole story, even in its details. Joseph "landed" in Pharaoh's officer's house, and then in a jail designed for the king's prisoners. Joseph could have felt that he was going further and further away from the dreams of his youth concerning the relationship with his family and his position of authority. But in reality he was getting closer and closer to God's plan. Joseph gained the proper behaviour, language and knowledge to relate to the poorest of the poor and the highest of the high ranking people in Egyptian society.

God's purpose in raising Joseph was more than Joseph

Joseph walked in the presence of very important people but his heart had been set free from the fear or the lure of men. He stayed faithful to God and His purposes. Some people are more excited to go before kings or presidents, high ranking officials or CEOs of international corporations, than to go before Jesus the KING OF KINGS. That was not the case with Joseph. His treasure was God Himself. His heart was free from the fear that men would make him lose something and free from covetousness to gain something that God had not given him. He was free to serve the purposes of God in his generation.

Joseph understood that the goal of God was not to make him famous or rich for himself (Luke 12:21). He knew that God had a kingdom purpose larger than his life because he was living before the King of Kings. Joseph understood that it was not about himself that he had been positioned in such a high place, but about God's people. He stated:

"... for God sent me before you ***to preserve life****."* (Genesis 45:5)
"... ***I will provide for you****, for there are yet five years of famine to come; lest you and your household, and all that you have, come to poverty.'"* (Genesis 45:11)

God raised Joseph to a place of authority, influence and wealth **to preserve the life of his people and to provide sufficient provision of food in a time of famine. His prosperity came with a responsibility**. Joseph was set to help the children of God, the Egyptians and the neighboring countries in order to avoid massive starvation. God's plan was larger than Joseph's wellbeing and promotion. He wanted to show His compassion to His creatures. If Joseph had been selfish, the rescuing Hand of God would not have reached the ones in need.

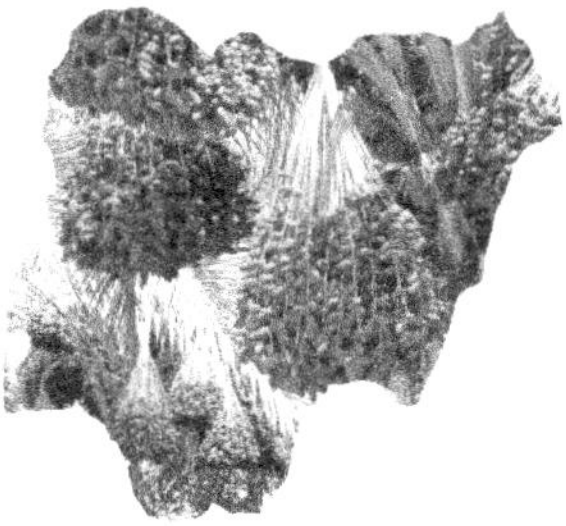

CHAPTER TWO

THE "JOSEPHS"

The "Josephs" are people that God has prepared or is preparing to **preserve life** in times of economic crisis leading to a lack of provision, and a lack of food for the poorest. Currently in Nigeria, according to the non-profit organization "Save the Children", there are little children, one to five years old, dying of malnourishment and related causes. The "Josephs" are raised up by God in such a time as this to provide for them and **preserve their precious little lives**.

Modern day "Josephs" are the ones that manifest Joseph's character. They are loyal to their authorities, trustworthy, honest and hard workers. They walk in integrity and sexual purity. They are men and women of truth. God is with them and they are with God. They cultivate a strong Bible-based relationship with Him and operate in the gifts of the Holy Spirit. They are problem solvers and solutions givers. Because they partner with the God who knows the future, they have the insights and the wisdom to bring solutions before the problem arises.

The **"Josephs" work hard to develop their skills and competence**. Each passing year they acquire more skills and abilities. They study without ceasing, they work hard to get new information, they explore new fields, they grow their knowledge, they attain expertise in their profession, they are interested in improving things, and they like to better themselves.

The "Josephs" are not selfish and self-centered. **They take the cause of the underprivileged to heart**. They are the ones working hard and giving sacrificially to support the little helpless ones. They love God and His children. The "Josephs" love to partner with God to see His purposes fulfilled on earth. Their reward is God Himself. **Their reward is to know that the Father in Heaven is pleased with what they are doing for His little ones**. Their reward is not to get rich for themselves but to use their God-given resources to alleviate the suffering of the poor.

The "Joseph" development of godly character

Although everyone loves the nine godly aspects of Joseph's character, it is a different reality to live them out on a daily basis and to attain this level of maturity.

Loyalty (or in other words faithfulness to authorities) will open a door for promotion. A boss will entrust more to a Joseph when he sees consistent and enduring loyalty. A loyal person is a rare pearl. The boss (like Potiphar), who has a loyal person as his manager, knows that his "Joseph" will not be divisive, will not talk behind his back, will not allow gossiping and will be a strong support for him in times of need.

A **trustworthy** person has **earned the trust** of his boss **by his steady faithfulness**. Some people complain that their boss does not trust them enough. But many times it is for a good reason. They have not shown behaviour that triggered trust. On the contrary, steadfast faithfulness will be welcome with a display of favor.

An **honest** person will be highly appreciated in every sphere of society. Honesty carries prosperity as history shows. The 16th century Reformer John Calvin transformed the poor, depraved, dissipated and dirty city of Geneva, Switzerland, into a center of prosperous trade by teaching honesty and integrity from the Word of God. Major hindrances to successful and fruitful business are dishonesty and corruption. Dishonesty slows down businesses. People are afraid to trade with dishonest people. They take a lot of precautions and cancel deals as soon as they feel they are being deceived, tricked or overcharged. On the contrary, an honest person or honest business attracts a lot of customers in the long-term because they feel safe and secure. Honesty boosts the speed of trade and increases the volume of transactions. Honesty and trust play a significant part in increasing the velocity (the rate at which money changes hands) that is so crucial to a thriving economy. Honesty is the best free advertisement. Satisfied customers will talk to their friends and bring in new customers, especially with the development of social media.

A **hard working** person like Joseph is a great asset to a company. On the other hand a lazy person is like a sink hole that swallows all the benefits. The sluggards are unable to complete a task and in their hands wealth disappears, as we can read in the Book of Proverbs. A boss can never rely on a lazy person, and finds himself helpless and distressed. My only advice to bosses that work with lazy people in their company is to sack them as soon as possible, because they will not be able to change their lazy ways. Lazy workers will make their business drown.

The "Josephs" walk in **integrity** and **sexual purity**. People who are not faithful to their spouse or are not afraid to interfere in someone else's marriage are the friends of the destroyer. They trample holy covenants as if they were nothing. In so doing they despise God and people. Joseph was afraid to offend God and to betray his master. Sexual harassment leading to adultery at work is a plague and should not be tolerated.

Joseph spoke **truthfully**. Lies destroy trust and relationships. They divide friends. God hates liars and will destroy them (Psalm 5:6). Truth builds. Lies lead only to destruction. Without truth leaders might make decisions based on misleading information, harming a whole business.

God was with Joseph and Joseph was with God. This point was the key of Joseph's many promotions. Sometimes people insist on competences, diplomas and accreditation (which is good) but they neglect the most important thing: **the manifest presence of God. This was the life changer in Joseph's life**. It is God who releases the blessing. It is God who makes everything fruitful and successful. Potiphar, the jailer, and Pharaoh saw the huge potential of "hiring" Joseph because God was with him. **Cultivate your relationship with God** to the point where people will tell you: God is with you. This is not secondary. This is the priority without neglecting the other aspects. Read the whole Bible every year (about 3-4 chapters a day). It will take you only 20 minutes daily. Study specific topics or books of the Bible on your own and attend Bible studies. Devote yourself to prayer and add some fasting from time to time. Sooner or later people will notice that God is with you.

The perseverance of the "Josephs"

Although everyone loves the end of Joseph's story, it was really tough to go through the lows and the highs of his life.

In God's training the "Josephs" will experience **perplexity and despair** several times on their journey. They will be tempted to give up their God-given dreams, and their faith will be tested through fire and water. If they do not receive instruction and encouragement from the Scriptures, their heart may fail (Romans 15:4; 1 Corinthians 10:11).

The "Josephs" should understand that God is with them and for them, not against them. It is not because they are doing something wrong that their whole world suddenly collapses, but because they are doing the right thing. Unlike the unrighteous ones who fall permanently, God always brings the righteous "Josephs" back to their feet and positions them higher. So "Josephs" do not be discouraged! You will end well and fulfill God's will in your generation.

The "Josephs" ongoing acquisition of skills

As we have seen, Joseph son of Jacob took every opportunity to get new skills. The "Josephs", likewise, should be determined not to let one year pass without acquiring new skills. From Joseph's life we see that **learning another language is important**. In today's global world, traveling will become more and more common. International trade will be increasingly significant. English is the most used and recognized business language in the world. The "Josephs" should aim at mastering this language as perfectly as possible. It will open doors of opportunities. Joseph spoke at least two languages fluently (Hebrew and Egyptian) but probably also Aramean, the language of his great grandfather Abraham. Which language should the "Josephs" learn? A simple observation of economic trends shows that Asia is surpassing America's economy. The number of billionaires and millionaires is increasing rapidly in the Asia-Pacific region. It could be wise to learn Chinese, 1.35 billion people speak Chinese, although with some regional variations. Other languages to consider learning are Korean or Japanese to be able to do business in or with these countries. In Europe the strongest economy is Germany, so learning German could be a good asset in the future. Of course, considering the African continent, French can also be useful to trade with French speaking neighboring countries. Currently half a billion people speak French on earth. Speaking two languages fluently will be an asset for the "Josephs". God will lead you to know which language you should focus on. **Mastering a** written and spoken **language**, even if you are gifted, **means hard work**.

Although he was a simple shepherd as a young teenager, Joseph developed **business skills**. He educated himself in **accounting and business planning**. He learned how to run a profitable business. He got informed about **international trading**. He got to know his product (grain) well. He found ways to **store and preserve food for many years**. The "Josephs" need to acquire basic knowledge about business and trade to be more successful. Every businessman should be familiar with some form of accounting, cost and margin calculation and business planning. They should gather a lot of information about the product they plan to sell or manufacture. They should be aware of similar products offered by other companies and compare prices and process of production. For example, you cannot start a production of solar systems without an extensive knowledge on the topic. Start small and simple and grow your business as you add to your current skills.

Obviously, **Joseph developed his spiritual skills and gifts**. It might come as a new idea to some people, but **God wants us to work on and sharpen our spiritual gifts**. For example, Prophet Samuel began a school for apprentice prophets (1 Samuel 10:5; 10:10; 19:20). In the time of Elijah the sons of the prophets were also gathered under the leadership of a "senior" prophet (Elijah and later Elisha 2 Kings 2:3; 2:5; 2:7; 2:15). Prophets need prophetic training, correction and coaching to reach maturity. The gifting is like a seed that matures into a tree. Every fruit tree needs pruning. A wild and unattended tree does not bear abundant and good fruit. Joseph received correction from his father Jacob about his dreams before being by himself in Egypt. There he had several opportunities to "test" his gift of interpretation of dreams before interpreting Pharaoh's dream. Apostle Paul was training the Corinthians to make good use of their gifts of the Spirit. It is not something that comes naturally. People who refuse to work on their spiritual gifting often bring embarrassment or even shame to the Body of Christ. I strongly encourage younger people to join a respected mature spiritual leader that will train them in his field of expertise.

Joseph developed his **leadership skills**. He was able to lead people well and achieve production goals. The "Josephs" should also work on their leadership skills by being with leaders, studying leadership models, observing successful leaders around them, and talking about leadership with people in these positions. But above all, they will gain tremendous insights by receiving leadership lessons from God, the Ultimate Leader, through His Word and His Holy Spirit. At an early stage, Joseph could oversee the employees and their work in the house of Potiphar; later he could oversee the overseers in the land of Egypt. Likewise when the "Josephs" reach the level to teach, they should then consider teaching teachers as they mature, grow in their expertise and be able to master more complex situations. Teaching teachers or training trainers is Jesus's model. It sets no limit to personal and to corporate growth.

Joseph had good **communication skills**. He was articulate, accurate and concise. Good communication is an effective tool in entrepreneurship and leadership. It allows a good communicator to cast a vision and to motivate people, to give simple and understandable assignments, to address authorities appropriately, to solve difficult work and personal conflicts, to negotiate prices with suppliers, employees or customers and much more. Joseph was also able to communicate well as he was not speaking his native language. The "Josephs" should work on their communication skills and perfect them. Although studying, learning and observing are all good, practicing is the best. A simple but effective way to improve communication skills is to request feedback from others. A simple question like: can you tell me what you understood? Can you please reframe what I just said? A good communicator often loves truth. Lies, hidden motives, secrets, and hypocrisy are often major obstacles to communication, because words are used not to convey a message but to hide things behind a "screen of smoke". Joseph spoke in truth and he enjoyed effective communication.

As **Joseph provided the solution before the problem** surfaced, the "Josephs" should work to have a **visionary mindset** and **divine wisdom** to be ahead of their time. If you are not a prophetic person, you can surround yourself with trusted prophetic people. And if you do not trust prophetic insights, you can study what the Bible says about the characteristics of the end-times. You can also look for mega trends in society to "foresee" the needs and challenges of the future. Observation allows us to see where things are going in many areas. Tomorrow solutions will be in the context of world globalization, mobility, and the information revolution (Daniel 12:4). Lack of food will also be prevalent in some geographical areas in the years preceding the return of Jesus (Mathew 24:7). Globally, the gap between the rich and the poor in society will become wider and wider, generating greater sufferings for the underprivileged. Sadly, slavery - with its misery - will come back, as it was in Egypt in Bible time (Revelation 6:15; 11:8; 13:6; 19:18). But if God finds an open ear to listen to Him, He will reveal His solutions that will alleviate the sufferings of His people because He loves them and wants to take good care of every one of His little ones in partnership with the "Josephs".

Five talents "Josephs" and two talents "Josephs"

Dear readers, some of you might be overwhelmed by the size of some of the skills development mentioned above. Please do not be discouraged, keep what is useful for your current situation. God gives to one person five talents, to another two, to another one, to each according to his ability (Matthew 25:15). Joseph, son of Jacob, was a five talent servant. His calling and task were proportionate to the size of an entire nation. Most of us will never reach this level of influence and we can be perfectly content with our God assigned portion. The important thing is to be faithful with what God has entrusted to us and to hear: "Well done, good and faithful servant; you have been faithful over a little, I will set you over much; enter into the joy of your master" (Matthew 25:21+23).

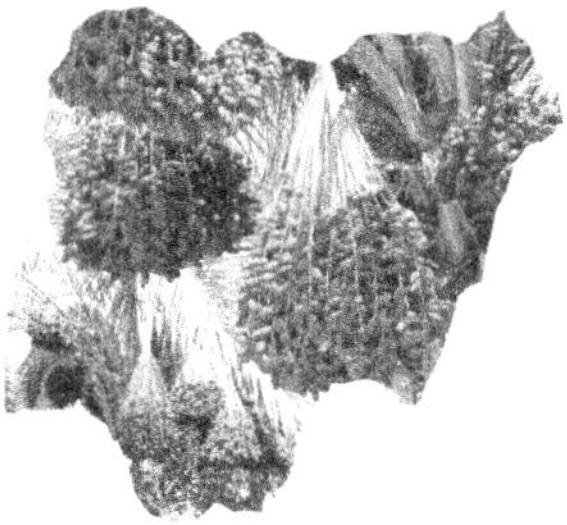

CHAPTER THREE

THE "JOSEPHS" BUSINESSES

T**<u>he number one need in a time of economic crisis is jobs</u>** and if possible well paid jobs or self-employment that pays. Like Joseph, become a job creator with the help of God the Creator who created the first job in the Garden before the Fall. There is a well-known say: "Give a man a fish, and you feed him for a day; teach a man to fish, and you feed him for a lifetime". All over the earth God is shifting the ways the church helps the needy: **<u>from charity to job creation</u>**.

<u>Note</u>: That is not to say that direct giving is not important in times of urgent need. Direct giving is a means of temporary rescue that has all its value, but job creation is a more durable way of transforming economic situations.

Modern day "Josephs" **<u>will provide work to others</u>** to rescue them from starvation. They might begin to create a job for themselves at first, but later they will grow their business and create other jobs. For example: A teacher can start a school and some years later offer jobs to other teachers. A salesman can grow his business and later he will need other local helpers. A carpenter can train young men to become carpenters and grow his business along the years. He will soon need the help of an accountant for his growing business and he will be ready to pay for his service.

If you think: "I can't create jobs", if you see problems rather than solutions, you might not be among the "Josephs" yet. That is okay. Find a "Joseph", help him and in so doing you will learn from him and acquire a "Joseph" mentality.

Do not wait for a "magic" effortless shortcut or an "anointing to get rich" because there are no such things. This is deception or childish fantasy. God's way is work, righteousness and generosity. He adds His blessing to multiply the fruit.

Joseph worked for Pharaoh, king of Egypt. The "Josephs" will work for their King Jesus. They will partner with God in their sphere of activity. **<u>They will involve God in their business and God will involve them in His business</u>**.

As "Josephs" you don't need to wait for Sundays to serve God. You can serve Him where you spend most of your time, and bring God's solutions into the needs of your community. You will be a blessing for others in the marketplace. You will become a problem solver releasing hope and provision for others.

God wants "Josephs" to run businesses that reflect the atmosphere and the values of His Kingdom. Among these values are faith, trust, honesty, integrity, loyalty, faithfulness, truth, service, competence, generosity and operating in the spiritual gifts. Here are some characteristics of the atmosphere of a Kingdom business: justice, peace and joy (Romans 14:17). Customers will feel safe dealing with such businesses. They will not fear being tricked, overly charged, or deceived.

Employees will also greatly benefit from being part of Kingdom businesses. They will enjoy a gossip-free zone at work and find support instead of criticism. They will grow in grace, forgiving others and being forgiven. They will not be required to lie or cheat to keep their job.

God knows and orchestrates the future (Pharaoh's dreams). He can inform His "Josephs" about what will be needed in the future that doesn't even exist today. God will inspire you and give you divine wisdom, creative ideas, innovative products or new services for your business that will add to what already exists in your area. He will also give you inventive ways of doing things or show you a specific need nobody has seen yet. Like Joseph God can give you information seven years ahead of other people. He is able to release a pioneering and visionary (prophetic) dimension within you combined with wisdom. God might give you dreams about what you have to begin. It will be significant and important to you. You will become passionate about it.

Once again, start small and simple, hold onto your faith and integrity, cultivate a deep Bible-based relationship with God, seek the guidance of the Holy Spirit, pray for wisdom, keep working hard, develop your skills, increase your knowledge, become an expert, and never despair when you go low. Guard you heart from the contagious infection of greed that might surround you, keep being generous and bless others.

Like Joseph, serve God in the marketplace with your gifts

"To **each** is given the manifestation of the Spirit for the common good" (1 Corinthians 12:7).

The clergy represents a maximum of 3% of the Body of Christ. God intends to activate 100% of His children to share His love. God made an abundant provision of spiritual gifts for His children. The efficiency of the Body of Christ in sharing God's love could easily be multiplied up to 33 times if everyone were involved.

Jesus does not necessarily need a member of the clergy to do his work, to help the poor, to perform a miracle, a healing, or give a word of prophecy. The **Spirit-filled "Josephs**" are able to do this according to their spiritual gifting.

Just picture how God envisions **the "Josephs" in mission**. On Monday a **Spirit-filled** taxi driver releases a word of knowledge to his unbelieving customer. On Tuesday the same person gets a prophecy from his hairdresser. On Wednesday his daughter receives healing through a Spirit-filled neighbor. On Thursday his wife receives a word of divine wisdom for her situation. On Friday the same family gets some practical help from compassionate Spirit-filled children of God. How long would it take to make them understand the loving care of God for them and to bring them all into the Kingdom of God?

A**<u>ll the spiritual gifts are given to show love</u>**: **<u>God's love</u>** and the **<u>love of the believers</u>**. The longest chapters describing the spiritual gifts in the Bible are in 1 Corinthians 12 and 1 Corinthians 14. The chapter that is in the middle, 1 Corinthians 13, talks about love. This means that **<u>the heart of the spiritual gifts is to demonstrate love</u>**. Jesus wants to use the "Josephs" to provide for his crisis-stricken children. He desires to manifest His love through them. God wants the poor to know that He cares. He did not create His children to be helpless victims but, after getting help, to become problem solvers for others. God wants to use the marketplace community to demonstrate His love.

"Joseph"'s businesses are profitable & serve the needs of people

The essence of business is to create wealth, to generate a profit and to serve people. Business people offer products or services that are considered valuable to the customer who will pay for it. A businessman adds value by his work to the product he bought, and he sells it to a higher price.

For example, a woman buys some flour, a few eggs, some sugar, a little bit of margarine and bakes a delicious cake. She paid much less for all the ingredients together than what she gets from her customers buying the ready-to-eat cake. It is her work that added value to the raw ingredients. Then, a salesman buys potatoes in the country and transports them to the city. The added value is due to the transportation and offering the product retail. Also, the customer does not need to go to the country to get his potatoes. He saves time, fuel and energy and he agrees to pay a little more for the potatoes. The salesman and the customer are both winners. Another example is a carpenter builds a doorframe and a door for a customer who does not know carpentry.

He sells the extra value of his "expertise" or competence. Likewise, a teacher sells her long-acquired knowledge to her pupils for them to be better prepared for the challenges of life. All these examples are win-win situations.

The business you start is linked to your gifts and skills

Make a list of all your gifts, competences, skills, abilities and resources. **Make another list of the need of the people in your community**. If you see that their need is food, be as specific and accurate as possible. Please do not write that they need food, but describe it: fresh vegetables, chicken, eggs or honey.

See if you can provide vegetables, chicken, eggs or honey. Maybe you can buy bees and let them work for you, then sell small jars of honey to your community. Perhaps you know how to grow vegetables and you have a relative that has a small plot of land; you can cultivate the most wanted vegetables on it and make a good profit. Observe how the list of your resources and skills can match the needs of your community. Imagine how you can start a Kingdom business to serve God and your people.

Maybe you are skilled in accounting and you see that many business owners are weak in accounting. You can offer them your services for a price. Some of you like computers and you see that some older people need to learn basic computer skills and are ready to pay for it. Perhaps you cook very well and some rich elderly people in your community are unable to prepare their meals every day. You know how to make the best bread in the area and you see that people like warm freshly baked bread. Moreover you know young people looking for a small job. You can hire them to deliver the bread at your customers' door.

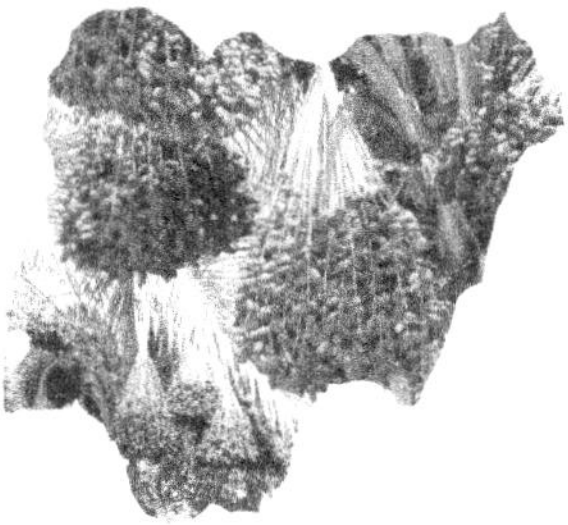

CHAPTER FOUR

THE UNSEEN RICHES OF NIGERIA: "JOSEPHS" IN THE MAKING

Here I will not talk about the rich high quality oil extracted from the Nigerian ground and sold all over the world. Neither will I speak about one of the best banking systems in the African continent.

I would like to talk about **the radiant and contagious faith of the Nigerian people**. I have been impressed by your love for God and your passion for His Son Jesus Christ. **You are known for operating in power evangelism, displaying the miracles of the Kingdom of God and for your dedication in prayer**. You have seen God answering you in impossible circumstances time and time again. Your faith is strongly established. With God you have confidence that everything is possible. And in this time of economic crisis it is still true. God will not let you down.

Like the Corinthian church that was filled with all the gifts of the Holy Spirit **you have been filled abundantly with spiritual gifts**. I have seen so many of you walking under the guidance and leadership of the Holy Spirit. Your spiritual life is "loaded" with dreams, visions, and divine insights. Your ministries demonstrate the power of the Holy Spirit in many ways. You have a living experience of the indwelling presence of the Holy Spirit. You know how it feels to have the Spirit of God moving within you. You know His motions and follow His leading. You are a people of the Spirit.

I also would like to mention **your love for life**. This is honoring the Creator, the living God, the Giver of life. You have many children and a very young population compared to the ageing inhabitants of Europe. You might see mouths to feed, and at times it might be overwhelming. I see a strong dynamic emerging generation ready to overcome the 21st century challenges.

You have taught your children to **respect authorities** and elderly people. This is an invaluable asset for the time before the return of Jesus. Without respect, the heart of the fathers cannot return to the heart of the children and the heart of the children cannot return to the heart of the fathers (Malachi 4:6). Without respect, the God-ordained winning combination of wisdom from the fathers and strength from the children cannot take place. In the West children have lost respect, and with it the support of their fathers. Although they have fathers, they are like a fatherless generation.

Your everyday life is not easy on a practical level but because of that you have become **strong, persevering and not easily discouraged**. You are not thin-skinned like the Europeans who tend to quit when it is getting tough. You have learned to fight until you see the victory.

S**olidarity** for your family and extended family is deeply rooted in your cultural DNA. I have even seen this sense of solidarity being extended to your villages or small communities. You still care for each other and have not been caught up in Western self-centeredness. You still know that you need each other for your everyday life and to achieve greater projects.

All these characteristics are the perfect seedbed to grow the rising "Josephs".

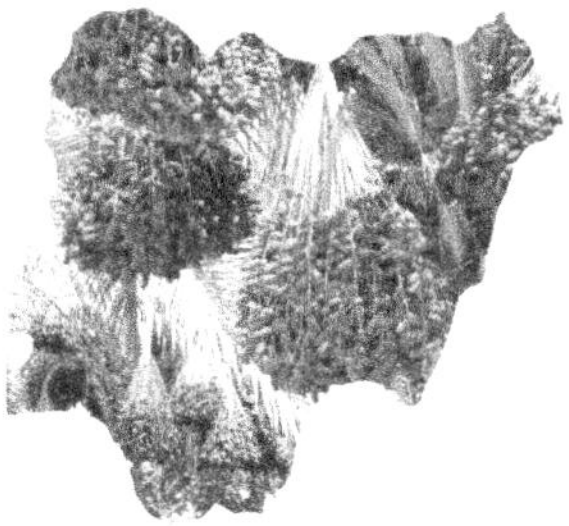

CHAPTER FIVE

RESTORING THE FOUNDATIONS

In the natural it is obvious that the infrastructures of Nigeria need improvement. The government officials, the business community and the general population are aware of that and work to improve the situation. The domestic water system needs to be repaired, sanitized and better supplied. The power stations of the country do not provide sufficient electrical power to Nigerian homes and businesses. The transportation of people and goods are hindered by a lack of safe highways, shortage of major routes and rare railroads. Very honorable efforts have been made along the years to improve these infrastructures. Everyone knows that it is a challenge to take care of the most populated country of Africa.

People operating businesses have become used to relying on their own solutions to secure sufficient water, electricity and broadband Internet connection. Many hotels and businesses have their own generator to supply their needs and those of their customers. Rich homeowners have also installed expensive alternative ways to secure their water supply, electricity and access to broadband Internet. Their tenacity in face of these difficulties is admirable.

But the less privileged members of the population do not have all these resources and do not see a way to run basic home appliances in their homes. Many people get sick from time to time because the tap water is not pure due to the lack of maintenance of old water pipes. If millions of homes could enjoy a steady supply of power and reliable tap water, a very profitable appliance market could open up and change the way of handling fresh food, dairy products and the washing of clothes and dishes.

Material infrastructures are like a parable of moral and spiritual foundations. In every nation moral and spiritual foundations come first, and then they are reflected in physical infrastructures. Many able, competent and good willed people have tried to improve the infrastructures and they have succeeded to a certain measure. But still, something like an invisible obstacle - like a grain of sand in the gears - has been hindering progress.

Many centuries ago, my country, Switzerland, was in dire poverty. The scarcity of food was such that men had to fight as mercenaries in foreign armies to keep their families from starvation. The Papal Swiss guards are a reminiscence of that very old past. The Swiss ground has no natural riches like oil, gas, uranium, rich minerals, diamonds or gold. The Bible teachings of the 16th century Reformers transformed the mentality and the behaviour of the population. Through the influence of the Reformers spreading in churches and the acceptance of biblical principles, Switzerland became known as a clean country of hard working people, honest trade, business integrity and trustworthy banking as well as the seat of many international humanitarian and political organizations working for peace.

Many people underestimate the role of moral and spiritual foundations in the building of a nation. Sin is like grains of sand in the gears of the system. Everything should work but it doesn't. But when the leadership and the population of a nation align with God's will, there are amazing results. God casts away the devourers of provision. He releases efficient solutions that people have been searching after for years without success.

According to the book of Proverbs, in an individual's life there are **four foundations of prosperity**: work, integrity, generosity and the blessing of God. There are also **four devourers of prosperity**: laziness, unrighteousness, standing surety and greed. These principles are also valid for a nation if they are correctly applied.

Laziness, unrighteousness and greed are like "black holes" swallowing all the fruits of prosperity.

One **lazy person** can ruin a whole project. The sluggard neglects his work and nullifies the work of the others (Proverbs 12:27; 19:24). He prevents the finalizing good deals. He is the brother of the destroyer (Proverbs 18:9). The sluggard refuses to work, diminishing the harvest and causing a shortage of food (Proverbs 20:4). He is a thorn in the flesh of his boss (Proverbs 10:26). Many good willed heads of departments are plagued with sluggards: they give orders but nothing is actually done! Lazy people neglect their work and waste the resources of others. They should be sacked and replaced by hard working employees. Sluggards are heading for poverty (Proverbs 6:6-11) and they pull others into poverty. On the contrary, hardworking individuals or nations are heading for prosperity. God will judge the slothful ones severely (Matthew 25:26-30).

U**nrighteousness** has many faces but I will address only two of them: unrighteous business practices and sexual unrighteousness. God hates false balances (Proverbs 11:1). He demands honesty in trade (Leviticus 19:35-36). He hates it when businessmen cheat and deceive others with false measures. God abhors people who take advantage of the misery of the poor to enrich themselves.

"4 Hear this, you who ***trample upon the needy****, and* ***bring the poor of the land to an end****, 5 saying, "When will the new moon be over, that we may sell grain? And the Sabbath, that we may offer wheat for sale, that we may* ***make the ephah*** *(= measure of quantity)* ***small*** *and the* ***shekel*** *(= the selling price in local currency)* ***great****, and deal deceitfully with false balances, 6 that* ***we may buy the poor for silver and the needy for a pair of sandals****, and sell the refuse of the wheat?""*

(Amos 8:4-6 RSV)

The prophet Amos exposes **unrighteous business practices**. The merchants trample upon the needy and oppress the poor of the land. They feel strong and mistreat the weak. They find ways to unnoticeably decrease the quantity and increase the price of their products. These merchants want to reduce the poor to economic slavery in order to take even more advantage of them. God hears the cry of the poor and He totally disagrees with the wickedness of these men. He will bring them to judgement. As a reminder, God-approved businesses are supposed to generate a profit and to **serve** the people and their needs.

A major hindrance to business development is **corruption**. Corruption casts an undesirable, bad image on a whole company, even if it is due to the malfeasance of only a few people. It brings discredit and disqualifies the business or the state-run department that accepts it. The corrupted person sees his/her own advantage in the short term, but his/her actions can bring the whole business down. A cheated and deceived customer will not be a returning consumer. A disappointed taxpayer will not be a returning voter. With the development of social media and customer reviews becoming the norm, companies that tolerate corruption in their midst are preparing their own funerals. No senior management should allow it to go on under their leadership. Corruption, that is undealt with, will eventually lead to business failure, or in state-run projects, to lack of needed resources for a large part of the population.

Today's access to instant and accurate online information helps identify corrupt practices very fast. Rather sooner than later corrupt employees will be exposed. Because of globalization customers, partnering companies and corporations have options. They do not depend on one company or one supplier any longer. They do not have to accept corruption as the only way to get services or products. The local, regional or national "monopoly" of one corporation is something of the past. People will look for other options in other parts of the world. The worldwide offers are numerous and the competition is intense. The most competent and honest corporations will have the largest shares of the market.

Sexual unrighteousness leads to poverty on an individual, corporate and national level. The Scriptures warn that sexual immorality leads to poverty (Proverbs 5:8-10; Luke 15:13; Luke 15:30).

"For by means of a whorish woman ***a man is brought down to a piece of bread****, and the adulteress will hunt for precious life."*
(Proverbs 6:26 KJ21)

The pornographic industry sucks billions of dollars from families every year. This huge amount of money could be used for much better purposes like buying food or furniture, improving homes, paying for medical expenses, financing an education for children, saving for a future car or future house, and so on. Statistics show that two thirds of divorces are related to sexual unfaithfulness. Divorces are a leading cause of pauperization in Europe as many divorced mothers have financial difficulties. States' social security systems are burdened to help them survive and take care of their children. Moreover, fatherless children are less likely to achieve high education and more likely to flirt with sinful or criminal activities (alcohol abuse, drug abuse, brawls, robbery and so on). Less prosperity or even poverty comes as a ripple effect. Divorced partners rarely reach their full prosperity potential. Sexual unrighteousness comes with a high cost for individuals, families, communities and even nations.

Sexual unrighteousness takes its toll on leaders. King Lemuel wrote about his mother's wisdom (Proverbs 31:1-9). She instructed him to not give his strength to women that destroy kings. History shows that powerful world empires have been taken down by sexual unrighteousness. The spirit of prostitution brings confusion and takes away understanding (Hosea 4:11; 4:12). King Solomon, having too many wives, was led astray. The God-given prosperity of his kingdom was never to be found again. Leaders who want to keep a clear mind to lead well abstain from sexual unrighteousness. Sexual immorality clutters understanding and sexual impurity numbs the soul. In turn this may affect the leader's ability to make right decisions that would benefit the wellbeing and prosperity of all that he was entrusted with. A simple example of this reality is how sexual unrighteousness debilitates the leadership of a husband. Also, a sexually unrighteous father will not be able to take good care of his children and will miss important decisions for their present and future wellbeing. **Sexual unrighteousness and good leadership are not compatible**. This is true on various levels of leadership.

G**reed** can be defined as the desire to acquire wealth in **larger amounts** and **more quickly** than God allows. Covetous people want to have a lot of money in the fastest way possible. Greed is a poison that destroys the one that it possesses (Proverbs 1:19) and bring trouble to his household (Proverbs 15:27). Greed might lead people to commit unrighteous and violent actions toward innocent people. Covetous people rob others of what is theirs. Their goal is their own benefit and not the common good. They use their strength or position to accumulate unrighteous gains. They live for today and do not think of tomorrow. For example, project managers might embezzle future investments or maintenance provision for their immediate pleasures. Greedy people can misappropriate considerable sums of corporate or governmental money for their own profit. This behaviour has disastrous effects on the long-term. The needed investments for the future are being diverted and there is nothing left when infrastructures need to be maintained or replaced. Greed carries its own destruction and brings poverty to many. The expected wealth for one or two turns out to be lack of provision for many.

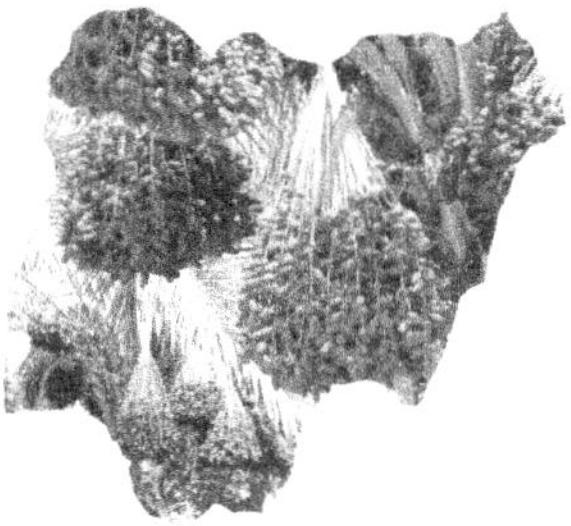

CHAPTER SIX

HOW COULD EVERYONE CONTRIBUTE TO ENDING NIGERIA'S RECESSION?

I would like to share briefly what every group's contribution could look like in this combined effort to restore Nigeria's economy.

The role of the ministers of God

Many times people do not pay too much attention to what God has to say. Each day is like another day and everybody goes to his business as usual. But a time of recession changes that. When the economy of a nation is not going well, people suffer. Then many questions pop up in the minds and hearts of the people: "What is going wrong? Is there something that we have to understand? Is God trying to say something to our nation?"

Now that **God has the attention of the nation**, what does He want to say?

Men are preoccupied with food and money to sustain their lives and they long to be restored to their previous level of prosperity. God is preoccupied with men turning from their sins and restoring righteousness in the land. God is so merciful. He is ready to forgive when He sees sincere repentance. He hates to see His children in pain. He aches with them in a time of economic distress. He longs to forgive but He waits for His children to return to Him with all their heart. He is ready to restore but He is looking for wholeheartedness.

The **book of Joel** describes four waves of locusts that leave the land famished and desolate. Each passing new wave brings the nation to a new level of poverty and despair. In addition to this plague, a severe drought increases the intensity of the famine in the land. The ministers of God are called to gather in the house of God, to lament and repent. Then they are to call all the inhabitants of the land to humble themselves, repent and ask God to spare his people (Joel 1:13-14; Joel 2:12-17). The message of Joel echoes the word God gave King Salomon on the inauguration day of the Temple (2 Chronicles 7:13-14).

God Himself gives the key to experience restoration as a nation. He does not leave His children in darkness. He tells them plainly what He is expecting:

*"12 "Yet even now," says the LORD, "**return to me with all your heart**, with fasting, with weeping, and with mourning; 13 and rend your hearts and not your garments." **Return to the LORD, your God, for he is gracious and merciful, slow to anger, and abounding in steadfast love**, and repents of evil. 14 Who knows whether he will not turn and repent, and leave a blessing behind him, a cereal offering and a drink offering for the LORD, your*

God? 15 Blow the trumpet in Zion; sanctify a ***fast****;* ***call a solemn***
assembly*; 16 gather the people.* ***Sanctify the congregation****;*
assemble the elders; gather the children, even nursing infants. Let
the bridegroom leave his room, and the bride her chamber. 17
Between the vestibule and the altar let the priests, the ministers of
*the LORD, weep and say, "**Spare thy people, O LORD**, and make*
not thy heritage a reproach, a byword among the nations. Why
should they say among the peoples, 'Where is their God?'" 18 Then
the LORD became jealous for his land, and had pity on his people.
19 ***The LORD answered and said to his people, "Behold, I am***
sending to you grain, wine, and oil, and you will be satisfied*; and*
I will no more make you a reproach among the nations."

(Joel 2:12-19 RSV)

God's ministers are called to lead "**Solemn Assemblies**" and "**National Days of Repentance**" **to lead people to turn from their sins to God**, and in so doing obtain again **divine favor** over the nation.

God is gracious and merciful. So much so that He gave His Only Begotten Son as a ransom for our lives. Jesus paid for our sins by offering his sinless life. There is no doubt that God wants to forgive. We can turn to Him in confidence: our repentance will be accepted.

In a National Day of Repentance, on a given day the nation agrees to turn to God, to repent collectively, to fast and to commit oneself to practice righteousness. As people gather to turn away from their sins and return to God, Heaven will notice. God will forgive, release His blessing and heal the land. A National Day of Repentance will be a significant step toward the restoration of Nigeria's economy.

The role of the "Josephs"

As the ministers of the Lord have cleared the way in the area of sin, now **the "Josephs" are able to bring practical solutions to the economy of the country**. They will use their God-given abilities to create jobs, share their expertise, offer counsel, generate opportunities, share resources, train and advise young entrepreneurs, develop new energetic strategies, innovate new services, encourage education and skill development, improve health attention to the poor, inspire new low rate micro credit lending and even present innovative ideas to advance transport lines and improve digital communication routes.

Because the "Josephs" have wise insights into the future, they are able to bring solutions ahead of the problems. Most of the "Josephs" will not operate on a national level but they will be able to implement the timely God-given solution in their communities. They will create businesses and job openings, generate wealth and release help to the malnourished children in their area.

However some "Josephs" called to operate on a national level will need the backing of the "Nation Builders", like Joseph, son of Jacob. He needed the backing of Pharaoh to implement his God-given strategies on a national level.

The role of the "Nation Builders"

The "Nation Builders" are a group of "super wealthy" people that will be ready to **invest** (for profit and in some cases as a gift) **in the main infrastructures** of Nigeria. Rich people usually dislike investing in unprofitable businesses or venues. Wealthy people loathe wasting their resources in enterprises that are not properly managed. Successful businessmen hate entrusting their hard-earned money into the hands of people that will waste, neglect or ruin their resources. The "Nation Builders" are upset when they observe how some ungifted people misuse money - money that other people have earned - in community projects. If, for example, they invest in a power station, they want it to be profitable, run properly, well maintained and generating good returns. Many of the "Nation Builders" have made their way up with a lot of hard work and sweat. They understand how much effort they had to make to be where they are. They do not want other people to misuse the money they have the responsibility to steward.

Wealthy people look for good investing opportunities with competent managers. They are ready to invest large amounts of money if they see a chance of success. Wealthy business-oriented people like to win, to gain money, and to turn things into great successes. They hate failure, inefficiency, and unprofitable companies. They do not want their name to be attached to mismanaged projects.

The combination of "Nation Builders" and "Josephs" can be a win-win situation, not only for both of them, but also for the whole country. They need each other to achieve great things for Nigeria. Pharaoh needed Joseph's wisdom, farsightedness and integrity, and Joseph needed Pharaoh's backing and resources.

The "Nation Builders" can invest in large projects that will benefit all, like opening **new routes for transport**. Goods and people will travel faster and more easily. Trade in the Roman Empire was boosted by **well-maintained axes of communication** like secured sea roads and safe land roads (like the Appian Way). Good, secure, reliable axes of transportation are key to interstates and international businesses. This has always been true in world history.

Maybe some "Nation Builders" will be interested in investing in private or semi-private **regional airports** (for domestic flights) to facilitate the coming and going of international business people. They themselves can greatly benefit by fast and reliable air transportation, to conduct and develop their companies in the different states of Nigeria.

As the population of Nigeria is very large and only a minority owns a car, it could be interesting to invest in secure and reliable **express railways** connecting large cities, since now private concessions are being made available. Neither regional airports nor railways can be the project of one man. In working together the "Nation Builders" could join their forces and contribute to improving the transport and communication system of the nation. Fast and dependable axes of communication will contribute to boost the economy and unite the large nation of Nigeria.

One "Nation Builder" could be willing to build a bridge or a tunnel to put an end to chronic traffic jams in a congested area of a town. The bridge could bear his name and his legacy could be remembered.

Some "Nation Builders" might also be interested in investing by connecting large cities with optic fiber to offer a **reliable network of high speed broadband Internet** connection. It could be a very profitable business and at the same time create a lot of jobs. The new Internet service could open new opportunities for businesses and the population in general, (like e-banking, e-commerce, e-trading, online training for the younger generation and access to crucial information for businesses and companies).

The "Nation Builders" could also be interested in developing environment friendly **solar power plants,** to offer a steady flow of electricity in some areas. In turn, the constant availability of power would generate new business opportunities and improve the wellbeing of the population in general. For example, a constant flow of power would encourage many people to buy home appliances to preserve food and to wash clothes and dishes. This would open a new very profitable multi-million customers market. In Europe the selling of electricity by private companies or individuals is now possible and the monopoly of state electricity has been deregulated. "Nations Builders" could also be highly motivated to invest in community or family solar systems as environment friendly solutions.

Some "Nations Builders" could be interested in improving and developing **the domestic water system** to provide a clean, reliable, constant flow of drinkable water to homes. In some parts of the world utilities companies are being privatized. The returns on the initial investments could be a stable and profitable source of income in the long-term.

Some "Nation Builders" would love to contribute to the **education of the younger generation**, establishing physical and **online libraries or learning centers** connected to broadband Internet. "Parental control" type of filters could be set in place to help students focus on their study and not waste their time and defile their purity by watching online pornography. The "Nation Builders" could create these online learning centers in large cities, in their native village, or close to where their grandchildren live. I have a wealthy neighbor who has already funded three elementary schools in rural Africa. She was so pleased to have done something good for others. Like this lady, "Nation Builders" often do not need money for themselves any longer but they would love to be helpful and lay a legacy for their countrymen.

Some "Nation Builders" would like to offer a **medical clinic** to their community and reduce the suffering of untreated diseases. There are so many opportunities to do good, and make a difference in these difficult times.

All these investments would create paid jobs and help hundreds or thousands of families. This is not about charity. It is about job creation that bolsters dignity and self-respect. Some of the "Nation Builders" have accumulated large amounts of wealth for such a time as this.

"Nation Builders" could be convened to take part in exclusive gatherings in which they could share ideas and join forces for their beloved nation.

The role of the "Community Builders"

The "Community Builders" are talented professionals ready to **share some of their professional expertise with the people in need in their community**. They might look like "Josephs" for their concerns for people and their love but unlike them they are not job creators, Kingdom business owners or strategic life preservers.

Giving is much more than transmitting money. **Sharing resources is a major way to give to others**. Sharing was the way the early church dealt with poverty and … "there were no poor among them" (Acts 4:32-34). Partaking enriches everyone and nobody gets poorer.

For example, doctors, ophthalmologists and dentists could give two hours every week to offer their professional care for free. The Bible shows that God is especially attentive to specific groups in need: widows, fatherless, foreigners and Levites (Deuteronomy 14:29; 16:13; 24:19; 26:11). Many widows, orphans, foreigners and pastors cannot afford good health care or dental care. It would be a big blessing for them to receive free care and God's blessing would surely return to the doctors, the ophthalmologists, and the dentists.

Ikewise, bankers could give free financial advice to the members of their community two hours a week. Mechanics could help people fix their car, computer specialists could debug and service someone's computer, lawyers could give free legal advice and teachers could teach for free for two hours a week. A cook could prepare extra portions for the family of the sick mother next door. Everyone can be a part of the "Community Builders" two hours a week and be a blessing to others. Sharing is the way of the Kingdom and it is a wonderful way to be generous when we have no money. Nobody gets poorer and everybody is enriched. Sharing is a win-win transaction. All the "Community Builders" will be richly blessed and will get many new friends. Love will flow! Love will ease the pain! Love will meet the distressed! Love will overcome despair! And God will be glorified! (Matthew 5:16). Solidarity is crucial in a time of crisis and it bears much fruit.

The role of police officers and law enforcement personal

The Bible teaches that people in authority are God's servants (or ministers of God). God empowers them to enforce justice and punish evildoers (Romans 13:1-5). They bear the sword, or weapons, to put the law into force. They represent the city, state or national government and they carry a delegated authority. Their uniform and weapons give them power. Everybody expects them to use their authority to make righteousness and goodness triumph. But sometimes some members of the law enforcement are tempted to use their authority for their own benefit.

During my last stay in Nigeria I flew into Lagos airport late in the evening and had to travel to a distant city during the night. A young armed police officer stopped our car and demanded to see my passport and my entry visa. I showed them to him and everything was in order. He suddenly confiscated my passport and told us to park the car on the roadside. I was told later that he was expecting to receive some money and that he would have never done that during daylight.

John the Baptist told the tax collectors who were state employees: "Collect no more than is appointed you", and to soldiers: "Rob no one by violence or by false accusation, and be content with your wages" (Luke 3:12-14). John the Baptist, the preacher of righteousness, told them not to use their official position to get some personal benefits.

It is a great honor to serve God as state officials, police officers and law enforcement personal. **God expects them to enforce justice and will bless them for that**. On the contrary, He will be displeased if they use their authority and power to take advantage of people. Righteousness creates a safe and secure environment for everyone that is very conducive to happiness, trade and prosperity.

The role of parents

It is impossible to overestimate the role of parents in a nation. They lay the foundations of success for the next generation. **They are the ones that first introduce God to their children** and then teach them to love Him with all of their heart. They are the ones that instruct them to love righteousness, practice mercy and walk humbly before the Lord. God appointed the parents first to pass on their knowledge of Him to their children (Deuteronomy 4:9). God places the responsibility to share His wonderful deeds into the parents' hands and only secondarily into the care of the churches.

Parents are the first to introduce their children to tender love. Their affection is the foundation of all their kids' future love relationships. Parental tenderness awakens love in the heart of the little ones. A father and a mother's love are unique and of high value. God entrusts so much to parents. Parents, your love will do miracles in the lives of your children. You are the ones contributing to their future exploits. Remember that Joseph's confidence in life was grounded in his father's love.

Parents are the only group of people that the Ten Commandments command us to obey. Children learn to obey God by first obeying their parents. They grow up by imitating their parents. Hardworking parents will have hardworking offspring. Honest fathers and mothers will have honest kids. Generous parents will have generous descendants. However, this principle might not be 100% accurate. There are exceptions to the rule because some children follow their own ways like Prophet Samuel' sons (1 Samuel 8:3).

Parents bless the God-given destiny of their children like Jacob did (Genesis 49). They confirm the God-given dreams living in the heart of their kids. They teach their offspring perseverance and never to give up. Godly parents are the primary "mould" to produce kind hearted successful "Josephs". They encourage them to study rather than waste their time in excessive entertainment or sinful activities. They instruct them to pray until the breakthrough comes. Parents are so precious to God. Their role is so central and essential.

R**eading the Bible as a family** is also a very important thing to do, as well as praying together at home. It will bring a lot of unity and generate many fruitful conversations. Studying specific topics of the Bible will help children make the right decisions as they grow and mature. For example, a teenager son will benefit greatly by reading and meditating on the book of Proverbs with his father.

The role of churches

C**hurches are places where we learn to love God**, as well as **the people that God has given us** as brothers and sisters.

L**oving God** is directly connected to **knowing who God really is**. God revealed Himself to His people through mighty exploits and by His anointed ones. From the beginning God has been interested to have friends (like Henoch, Noah, Abraham, Moses and David) whom He told who He is. God loves relationships. He likes to be a Friend and a Father. God wants to be known. We do not need to guess who God is. Ultimately God made Himself known in Jesus His Son. Jesus has shown us the Father. He is the perfect representation of the Father. He has given us access to Him. Jesus has set us free from the misrepresentations of God. We can now love Him with all our heart and strength. Making God and His Son known and loved is one of the major roles of the churches.

History shows that major transformations in individuals, in families and in nations take place when the Bible is studied under the inspiration of the Holy Spirit. The revelation of God in the Scriptures under the leadership of the Holy Spirit renews the mindset and the worldview of the people. This can transform a nation for the best.

God designed the Body of Christ to be diverse, uniting rich and poor, educated and less educated, black and white, male and female, Jew and Gentile and young and old to teach us how to **love His children**. His grand purpose is to unite people that are different, yet they are all His children around His precious Son Jesus. Without churches we can easily meet only people like ourselves. Congregations are places where we are reminded that God loves all His children as much as He loves us. **It is His family. It is our family**. Solidarity and family go hand in hand. God designed the family to be a place of love, something that nothing can buy. Family is not about money but about love.

Churches are places where we learn the economy of the Kingdom, the reality of love, which is giving and receiving. The economy of the world is about buying and selling. Both have their place in the plan of God. But what would the world look like if love had no place to reign? What would the world be if money ruled everywhere?

The role of media

People in the media initiate a lot of conversations in the country. The population think and talk about what they have heard, read or watched. God-given mandate to the media is best summarized in this one sentence from Apostle Paul:

*"Finally, brethren, whatever is **true**, whatever is **honorable**, whatever is **just**, whatever is **pure**, whatever is **lovely**, whatever is **gracious**, if there is any **excellence**, if there is anything worthy of praise, **think about these things**."*

(Philippians 4:8)

The media set much of the tune of the discussions and preoccupations of the country. The people of Nigeria need truth, honor, justice, purity, love, grace and excellence to feed their thoughts. Of course, there are ugly things going on in the world that need to be mentioned for the sake of truth, but they should not take all the attention. There are also useless or dishonorable media-generated preoccupations that clutter the mind of people like covetousness, envy, violence, self-centeredness or lust. **The media need to report and focus on what is true, honorable, just, pure, and excellent and then the population will think about these things**.

People working in the media have their God-given role to play in elevating the soul of their audience and contributing to the edification of the Nigerian people. They can use part of their program to share stories of integrity and success, merit and amazing achievements, compassion and purity. They can sow honorable role models that will inspire the younger generation to aim for excellence. The media can contribute to "water" the seeds of "Josephs" in Nigeria.

The role of artists

God created artists to convey beauty and joy, to elevate souls and to help people share deep feelings and emotions. The true calling of artists is to give glory to God and invite their audience to encounter Him in their circumstances. The most famous masterpieces in history are often linked to exalting the wonderful deeds of God in creation or in redemption (Handel's Messiah; Michelangelo's Creation of Adam; Rembrandt's Return of the Prodigal Son).

Music is very popular in Nigeria and probably singers and musicians are the most well-known artists in the country (above actors and painters). **Their music and songs can convey hope, faith, light and beauty** or on the contrary despair, fear, darkness and impurity. These artists can encourage their audience to go higher and choose love, solidarity and unity or to go lower and choose selfishness, rebellion, sin and indifference.

God's gift to artists is to let them feel what other people experience. Sometimes too He lets them feel His emotions in that same situation. In the current recession, Nigerian artists might express the deep feelings of the needy and their suffering, but it is also their responsibility to let God's light shine and bring hope in these difficult times. God has in store some songs that will convey hope, faith and love to the whole nation of Nigeria. He will release them to the artists that are willing to listen to Him and serve Him with their God-given musical gifts. They will be a blessing to their nation.

The role of teachers

Teachers have a glorious, yet scary, responsibility toward children. They teach them basic knowledge but they also share their perspective on God, life and the world with their pupils. The students learn to see God, humanity and history through their teacher's eyes. Parents and teachers have a different yet complementary role in the upbringing and education of children. The first information received leaves a strong print on the mind of these young ones. What is learned early in life often remains unquestioned. Sadly, atheistic governments have understood this principle and used the school system to "purge" their nation of the fear of God.

The Word of God states that teachers will be judged more severely (James 3:1) because of their influence on their listeners. This principle first applies to Bible teachers but it is also valid for school teachers. Every one of them should be aware of the responsibility he/she carries for the life of his/her students.

It is crucial that **teachers bring God's perspective on every topic taught at school**. The study of anatomy and its complexity should kindle praise looking at the genius of the Creator. Mathematics and physics are connected to the wisdom of the One who designed a coherent and well-ordered world. History is His Story, showing how God leads the nations. Learning about astronomy should leave the students in awe of the infinite majesty and grandeur of their Creator. Studying foreign languages and cultures should reveal the passion of God for diversity and His desire to reach out to all humanity.

Teachers lay the foundations of the basic knowledge and skills for future "Josephs". **They encourage studying and learning**. They strengthen healthy curiosity and inspire new discoveries. They open doors for further explorations into unknown territories. They share their love for wisdom and their passion for learning. Teachers are an inspiration and a model for the "Josephs" who are eager to learn. Their God-ordained contribution for a prepared generation of "Josephs" is huge.

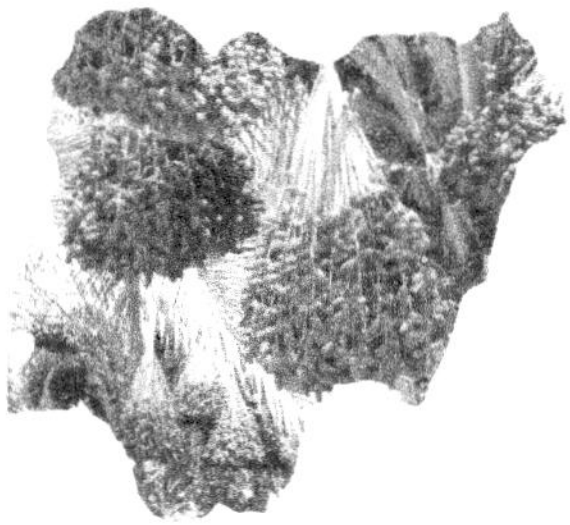

CHAPTER SEVEN

GOD AND MONEY

A biblical perspective on the stewardship of money

A lot of finance will go through the hands of the "Josephs" and it is important to have a biblical perspective on the stewardship of money. The conscious or unperceived love of riches is a snare for many people. They begin well but do end not so well.

Joseph, son of Jacob, learned to steward the wealth of others faithfully. **The "Josephs" will have to steward the money that God entrusts to them and use it according to His will**.

But first, let's go to the next paragraph and have a good laugh...

"The silver is mine, and the gold is mine, says the LORD..."

(Haggai 2:8)

A few years later ...

Whose wealth is it in reality? Is it really God's? Is it God's money only when we can receive it? Is it also God's wealth when He is asking us to give it away?

"17 Beware, lest you say in your heart, '<u>My</u> power and the might of
<u>my</u> hand have gotten me this wealth.' 18 You shall remember the
LORD your God, ***<u>for it is He who gives you power to get wealth</u>****;*
that He may confirm His covenant which he swore to your fathers,
as at this day."

(Deuteronomy. 8:17-18)

God is the owner, we are His stewards

It is easy to say that silver and gold belong to God when we do not have any money. But when we do have money, are we ready to say that silver and gold belong to God? Do we change our "declaration of faith" according to our financial situation?

Truly money belongs to God all the time. He is the owner. We are His stewards. **God likes to do what He wants with His money**. He does not want us to do what **we** desire with His money. **Have you ever tried to do what you wanted with the money of your boss?** If you did, you surely regret it today. You might remember how angry he was and how afraid you were when everything was exposed. It is the same with God.

We are only stewards of God's wealth & He holds us accountable

*"42 And the Lord said, "Who then is the faithful and wise **steward**, whom **his master** will set over **his household**, **to give them their portion of food** at the proper time? 43 Blessed is that servant whom his master when he comes will find so doing. 44 Truly, I say to you, he will set him over all his possessions. 45 But if that servant says to himself, 'My master is delayed in coming,' and begins to beat the menservants and the maidservants, and to eat and drink and get drunk, 46 the master of that servant will come on a day when he does not expect him and at an hour he does not know, and **will punish him, and put him with the unfaithful**. 47 And that **servant who knew his master's will**, **but did not** make ready or **act according to his will**, **shall receive a severe beating**."*

(Luke 12:42-47 RSV)

God expects His stewards to give their portion of food to the members of His household. In so doing the stewards will be approved and blessed. But if they use their

Master's resources for themselves ("to eat and drink and get drunk") and abuse others, they will be punished.

God is the owner. It is His household, His food, His possessions and His wealth that He wants us to distribute. We cannot do what we want with what is His (and not ours). The devil's deception is to make us believe that the wealth, the gifting and the strengths we enjoy are ours. **Everything is God's**. We have received everything from Him and we are only stewards, never owners. The good steward acts according to the Master's will. The evil one overfills himself with food and drink and he mistreats the other servants of the Master. He acts in a selfish way and God holds him accountable.

During worship we sometimes sing or declare: "I am yours. You have redeemed me. I belong to you, Oh, God, my life is yours." But suddenly, when it comes to our wallet, we consider it our own. Do we not deceive ourselves? The devil likes to make us think that what we have in our hands is "our money". The truth is that it is the wealth that God has entrusted to us. It will always be His money, never ours.

God's heart for the poor

As Jesus begun his ministry, he quoted the Isaiah 61 prophecy and declared:

*"The Spirit of the Lord is upon me, because **he has anointed me to preach good news to the poor**. He has sent me to proclaim release to the captives and recovering of sight to the blind, to set at liberty those who are oppressed, to proclaim the acceptable year of the Lord."*

(Luke 4:18-19 RSV)

G**od sent His Son first to the poor**. God thought of them first. The Good News is first for the poor, including the widows, the orphans, the sick and the oppressed. In society they are always last, but they are first in the mind and heart of God.

"12 For he (God) delivers the needy when he calls, the poor and him who has no helper. 13 He has pity on the weak and the needy, and saves the lives of the needy. 14 From oppression and violence he redeems their life; and ***precious is their blood in his sight****."*

(Psalms 72:12-14 RSV)

God pays close attention to the lives of the poor. Many times in their distress they feel forsaken by God. But He is near them. He hears their cries. The blood, meaning the life of the poor is precious to God. He is the defender of the poor. The haughty think that they can trample the poor because they are helpless. But God delivers them from oppression.

According to the humanitarian association "Save the Children", currently small children are dying of malnourishment and related diseases in Nigeria. God is not okay with that. Precious is their blood in His sight. He wants some of His money to be used to rescue them and give them a future. He expects His stewards to use His money as He is directing them. God will richly reward those who do His will (1 Timothy 6:17-19).

The money entrusted to the "Josephs" has a goal that is to **preserve life** in a time of famine. The God-given successes of the "Josephs" are not to pump up their ego or their bank accounts. They have been given resources to help the little ones survive. Do not misinterpret your promotions. They have a much larger purpose than you. **God is raising "Josephs" to be kind, compassionate, tender hearted rich people, who will be ready to be His hands reaching out to His precious little ones**.

This book was completed at Christmas 2016.

*""**Glory to God** in the highest, and on earth **peace among men with whom He is pleased**!""*

(Luke 2:14)

APPENDIX: PRACTICAL SUGGESTIONS FOR MODERN DAY "JOSEPHS"

- Get acquainted with **new technologies** and see how they can be beneficial to your business (computers, software, website creation, web design, online business, online advertising, mobile technologies, social media, solar systems, drones, e-resources, e-commerce, e-banking, and so on).
- Get informed about the **new trends** in society and see if you can start a profitable business (health, nutrition, fitness, gym, body care, personal sports coach, and so on).
- Observe the rise of "**green**" solutions (garbage sorting, recycling, environment friendly approaches, renewable sources of energy, pollution free systems, water filtering, and so on).
- Get information on new management software for large corporations or large government structures. **Speed** is the most wanted feature to assure efficiency, advance and supremacy. Large organizations hate to waste time and resources. They are looking for new ways to do their task effectively. There is a race for computer speed among the most advanced nations. For example, Japan has budgeted $173 million to build a supercomputer in order to have the world's fastest machine in 2018, surpassing China and America.
- If you are a builder or a contractor you might follow the **mega 3D printer** development. China has recently been building numerous and inexpensive houses in a few days with the help of huge 3D printers pouring concrete with additives. This new technology allows constructing the

walls of a house in one shot from foundations to roof with openings for the doors and windows as well as the connections for the electrics and the plumbing.

- If you are a young person, **study how to prepare for job interviews** to increase your chance of being hired (how to greet your potential employer, how to dress, how to speak verbally and non-verbally, what to say about yourself, how to prepare your CV and highlight your résumé and so on).
- If you are still young and have not been able to graduate from a trade, do not give up, attend lectures, get trained and **graduate**. Your graduation will be an asset for your future.
- With ongoing inflation and the possible prospect of hyperinflation, study how to **negotiate a pay raise** with your employer, to protect your family's means of living.
- If you are in real estate, get informed about the **new trend of online visits to properties** with video streaming, 360° tours, professionally staging the house and the use of social media in your field of expertise. In today's mobile world, buyers can show up from anywhere on the planet. The time of neighbors buying the next door house is mostly over.
- If you are interested in bringing your contribution to **food production** for your country, get information on agriculture and how to grow crops, vegetables, fruit, bushes, trees or flowers most effectively. It is important to optimize your results with the latest improvements and know the potential markets. Get information on **new hydroponic technologies** and their very profitable combination with a fish farm. God has blessed Nigeria with a rich combination of sun, warmth and abundant rainy seasons. **The climate is very conducive to agricultural growth**. Food will always be the first vital need and trends show that as the price of manufactured goods have been falling, the price of food has been rising steadily.

- Getting some information on wood production and **forestry** might be beneficial. Even with the variety of new synthetic materials, **lumber** will continue to be used in construction and wood in paper production. Beautiful tropical wood will certainly sell at high prices to produce hand crafted furniture or pieces of art.
- There is a huge potential **milk market** in Africa. It is possible to have highly productive milk cows on African soil. This market well serves the nutritional needs of the people, and raising cattle is a more direct way to work hand in hand with the Creator, like the patriarchs did.
- **Solar systems** might be one of the answers to provide a steady flow of electrical power to homes or to communities. Nigeria has so much sun and it is for free! Some solar systems are designed to be installed on the roof tops of individual homes. They can be linked with a battery that will be charged during the day and release power through the night. Solar panels on a roof can provide enough energy for light duty (fans, lights, phones, laptops, some small energy saving fridges) but not for heavy duty (AC, washing machines, dishwashers, freezers). The solar industry and the battery industry improve their products very fast producing new possibilities every year.
- **Propane operated fridges** could also be an alternative in places where solar power is not yet available.
- Rice is a basic food in Nigeria and much rice is imported from abroad at high prices because of the current currency exchange rate. Exploring **indigenous rice plantations** and indigenous rice production could be a good idea in the coming years.
- Certifying a **network of trusted businesses** could also be very productive and profitable.

ABOUT THE AUTHOR

Born in 1962 in French speaking Switzerland, Pierre Bezençon encountered the Risen Lord in 1979. He got married in 1983 with Laurence.

Pierre and Laurence Bezençon obtained a Master's degree in Theology in 1987 (University of Neuchâtel). They have been in full-time ministry since 1988. They founded and have been leading "Foyers d'Amour" (Homes of Love) since 1999, a Bible training center geared towards leaders and couples. They also started a congregation in 2000 with a special emphasis on revival, prayer and mission.

Pierre Bezençon was ordained as an apostle on February 29th 2004 in La Chaux-de-Fonds, Switzerland. Since then, his teaching ministry has led him to several nations in Africa to train and equip church leaders.

Pierre and Laurence Bezençon live in Switzerland and in Kansas City, Missouri, where they join the life of the International House of Prayer (IHOPKC).

In 2009 beside his ministry, Pierre Bezençon started a small business, renovating and renting out houses in Kansas City, Missouri, USA.

Pierre Bezençon's favorite teaching themes are God's fatherhood, the extraordinary identity of Jesus, fellowship with the Holy Spirit, apostolic reformation, messianic reformation, administration of the prophetic, edifying the church according to the divine model and all that concerns the life of couples and the role of husbands and men.

Pierre Bezençon wrote three books:

- On a pris mon Seigneur (They Have Taken My Lord)
- Mon Père et votre Père (My Father and Your Father)
- Lasting Prosperity, Financial Wisdom from the Proverbs

He recorded several teachings for men and for leaders as well as a one year Bible overview: "Bâtir sur le Roc" ("Building On the Rock").

CONNECTING IN NIGERIA

Since 2013 Pierre Bezençon has been invited in Nigeria to speak in Pastors' conferences on Hearing the Holy Spirit, The leadership of Jesus and The Heart of God. He also spoke in two marriage seminars and one business people conference.

Pierre Bezençon encourages pastors to hold Solemn Assemblies. He has been praying for a National Day of Repentance to take place in Nigeria.

connecting with Facebook : JOSEPHS NIGERIA

To be informed or for enquiries about our conferences and events: Text or call 09057116666.

Made in the USA
Monee, IL
04 November 2026

67380118R00046